I0814284

WEIRD WORLD

WEIRD MOMENTS IN HISTORY

BY EMMA KAISER

Core Library

An Imprint of Abdo Publishing
abdobooks.com

Cover image: In the mid-1900s, many sightings of alien spacecraft were reported in the United States. The most famous is remembered as the Roswell incident.

abdobooks.com

Published by Abdo Publishing, a division of ABDO, PO Box 398166, Minneapolis, Minnesota 55439.

Printed in the United States of America, North Mankato, Minnesota.
102025
012026

Cover Photo: Ted Soqui/Sygma/Getty Images
Interior Photos: Shutterstock Images, 4–5, 17 (wave), 17 (house), 17 (person), 34–35, 36; Granger, 7; Prisma/Universal Images Group/Getty Images, 9; Anibal Solimano/Getty Images News/Getty Images, 10; Leonardo Fernandez/Getty Images News/Getty Images, 12–13; Photo Josse/Leemage/Corbis Historical/Getty Images, 15; Ivan Kuzmin/Adobe Stock, 20–21; Stock Montage/Archive Photos/Getty Images, 22; DEA/Icas94/De Agostini Picture Library/Getty Images, 24, 43; Missouri Historical Society, 26–27; Ken Griffiths/Shutterstock Images, 28; Kean Collection/Hulton Royals Collection/Getty Images, 31; Fine Art/VCG Wilson/Corbis Historical/Getty Images, 32, 45; Matthew James Ferguson/Shutterstock Images, 39

Editors: Riley Madsen and Katharine Hale
Series Designer: Marley Richmond

Library of Congress Control Number: 2025939323

Publisher's Cataloging-in-Publication Data

Names: Kaiser, Emma, author.
Title: Weird moments in history / by Emma Kaiser
Description: Minneapolis, Minnesota: Abdo Publishing, 2026 | Series: Weird world | Includes online resources and index.
Identifiers: ISBN 9781098298494 (lib. bdg.) | ISBN 9798384932291 (ebook)
Subjects: LCSH: Oddities--Juvenile literature. | History--Juvenile literature. | History in popular culture--Juvenile literature. | History and anthropology--Juvenile literature. | Curiosities and wonders--Juvenile literature.
Classification: DDC 909--dc23

CONTENTS

CHAPTER ONE

CURIOUS COINCIDENCES

John Adams and Thomas Jefferson were the second and third presidents of the United States. On a July day in 1826, they were both ill and confined to bed. They were hundreds of miles apart in different states. But they were still in each other's thoughts.

Adams and Jefferson are considered founding fathers of the United States. They worked together to draft the Declaration of Independence. They also worked as diplomats to persuade France to help the United States win the Revolutionary

Along with Thomas Jefferson, *right*, and John Adams, *center*, Benjamin Franklin, *left*, also helped draft the Declaration of Independence.

THE BIRTH AND DEATH OF MARK TWAIN

Mark Twain was a famous author. He is known for his novels *The Adventures of Tom Sawyer* and *Adventures of Huckleberry Finn*. Twain was born in Missouri in 1835. The night of his birth, Halley's Comet passed over Twain's hometown. This comet passes near Earth about every 75 years, becoming briefly visible to the naked eye. Twain remained fascinated by the comet his whole life. He famously predicted that because he was born under Halley's Comet, he would die under it too. The comet made its next visible approach to Earth on April 20, 1910. Twain died of a heart attack the next day.

War (1775–1783) against Great Britain. And they both served as leaders of their new country.

Yet the two men had an unlikely and sometimes strained friendship. They were different in many ways. Adams came from a middle-class background. Jefferson was considered higher class. They disagreed over many political issues. Jefferson was quieter and more reserved. Adams was more passionate.

Monticello, Thomas Jefferson's home where he died, was completed in 1809. The building still stands today and is a museum of Jefferson's life.

They were even opposite in appearance. Jefferson was tall and thin, while Adams was short and stout.

Both men ran for president in 1796. It was a close race, but Adams won. In 1800, they both ran for president again. This time, Jefferson won. The two men

THREE-TIME SURVIVOR

Violet Jessop was born in 1887. She worked as a stewardess and nurse on ocean liners. These ships carry passengers across oceans. Jessop worked on three very famous ships, the *Olympic*, the *Titanic*, and the *Britannic*. These were sister ships. This meant they were made using nearly identical designs. All three ships had disasters with Jessop on board, and she survived each time. A warship ran into the *Olympic* in 1911. No one was injured, but both ships were badly damaged. The *Titanic* famously sank in 1912 after it hit an iceberg. The *Britannic* sank in 1916 due to an explosion. Jessop continued working as a ship stewardess until 1950.

did not speak to each other for 12 years. Finally, Adams broke the silence by writing a letter to Jefferson. Jefferson responded. They then exchanged 158 letters over the next 14 years.

Jefferson died at age 83 at his home in Virginia. Adams died at age 90 in Quincy, Massachusetts. They both died within a few hours of each other on July 4, 1826. It was the fiftieth anniversary of the signing of the Declaration of

Fifty-six people signed the Declaration of Independence, including Adams and Jefferson.

Independence. Adams's last words were reported to be, "Jefferson still lives."

STUDYING HISTORY

History is the study of the past. Sometimes history allows people to recognize patterns in human behavior. Sometimes it helps explain how things in the present came to be. History gives insights into how politics, economics, culture, and art evolved over time. But some moments in history are incredibly weird.

Archaeology is the study of ancient people and the objects from their lives. Peruvian archaeologist Sonia Guillén, *right*, has made many interesting discoveries in her career, including mummified remains of both people and dogs in Peru.

Two US presidents both dying on the fiftieth anniversary of their country's founding is a coincidence that still interests historians today. Plenty of other moments in history stand out as coincidental or weird. Sometimes these moments are events that affect only a few people's lives. Sometimes they can affect the whole world. These kinds of weird moments can make history especially interesting to study.

STRAIGHT TO THE SOURCE

After 12 years without speaking, John Adams broke the silence by writing to Thomas Jefferson on January 1, 1812. He wrote:

> *Dear Sir,*
>
> *. . . All of my Family whom you formerly knew are well. My Daughter Smith is here and has Successfully gone through a perilous and painful Operation, which detains her here this Winter, from her Husband and her Family at Chenango. . . .*
>
> *I wish you Sir many happy New years and that you may enter the next and many Succeeding years with as animating Prospects for the Public as those at present before us. . . .*
>
> *John Adams*

Source: "From John Adams to Thomas Jefferson, 1 January 1812." *National Archives*, n.d., founders.archives.gov. Accessed 17 Apr. 2022.

CONSIDER YOUR AUDIENCE

Adapt this passage for a different audience, such as your principal or friends. Write a letter conveying this same information for the new audience. How does your letter differ from the original text and why?

FOOD FOLLIES

Food has a strong connection to history. The foods people grew and ate can tell historians a lot about past societies. The search for food has also inspired important historical events. For example, Europeans' desire for East Asian spices led Christopher Columbus to seek a new route to India. He ended up in the Americas. There he was introduced to new foods such as potatoes.

Potatoes were first cultivated by the Incas in what is now the country of Peru. When Spanish explorers traveled to Central and South America,

A Peruvian farmer shows off a purple potato. Peru is home to the International Potato Center and the Potato Park. These organizations work to protect different potato varieties.

they ate these starchy root vegetables for the first time. They brought potatoes back to Europe in the 1500s.

While potatoes slowly spread to the rest of Europe, they were not popular. This was especially true in France. French people refused to eat potatoes. They believed potatoes caused illnesses and were bad for people. The French government even banned potatoes in 1748.

French pharmacist Antoine-Augustin Parmentier was determined to prove everyone wrong. He had eaten many potatoes and had not become ill.

FRENCH FRIES?

Some people believe that french fries actually came from Belgium. Others argue that they came from France, as their name implies. Fried potatoes may have been sold by French street vendors in the late 1700s. Thomas Jefferson is said to have brought fries to the United States. An 1802 White House dinner had "potatoes served in the French style" on the menu. French-fried potatoes became popular by the 1870s. Over time, the name shortened to *french fries*.

Antoine-Augustin Parmentier holds a bouquet of potato flowers, wheat, and corn in this painting by François Dumont. Parmentier first ate potatoes while a prisoner of war during the Seven Years' War.

He wanted to convince people that potatoes were healthy and tasted good. Parmentier performed research that showed potatoes were nutritious. He also helped reverse the ban on potatoes. He held elegant dinners where he served potatoes and invited famous guests. He gave the French king and queen a bouquet of potato flowers. But the French people were not convinced.

Parmentier tried another tactic. He turned a plot of his land into a potato patch. Then he hired armed men to guard the patch. Parmentier thought if people saw the guards, they would assume whatever grew there was valuable. Parmentier told his guards to allow people to steal the potatoes. He also told them to accept bribes if people offered them. Soon, more and more people started stealing potatoes from the patch.

Potatoes became more popular. By 1795, people began to plant huge fields of potatoes. The potatoes fed the French people when food was scarce. Today, several French potato dishes are named after Parmentier.

THE GREAT MOLASSES FLOOD

While an abundance of food is usually a good thing, in some weird cases, it can also be dangerous. This was true for the people of Boston, Massachusetts, on

HOW TALL WAS THE GREAT WAVE OF MOLASSES?

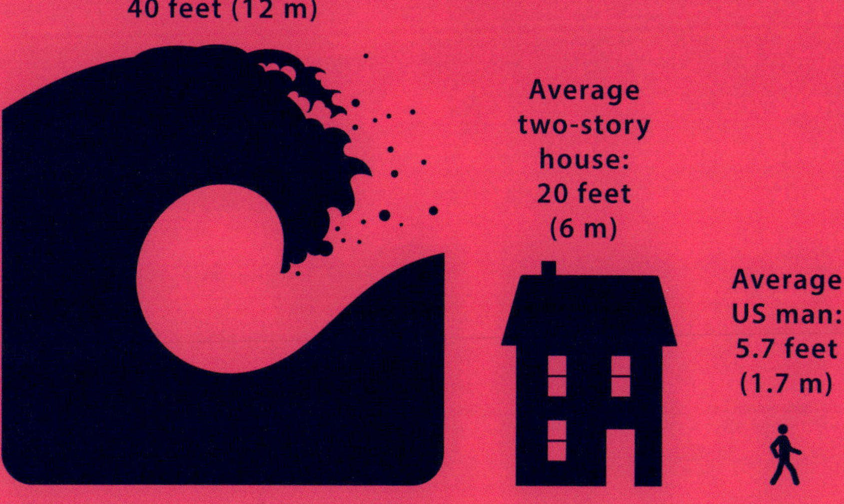

The tallest height reached by the wave of molasses during the Great Molasses Flood was 40 feet (12 m) high. How does this compare to the height of other things potentially affected by the flood?

January 15, 1919. That day, the north end of Boston was flooded with molasses. This is a thick, sticky type of syrup. The flood occurred when a very large storage tank broke open. The tank was 50 feet (15 m) tall and held 2.3 million gallons (8.7 million L) of molasses. This event became known as the Great Molasses Flood.

THE KENTUCKY MEAT SHOWER

In 1876, a couple from Bath County, Kentucky, watched a strange substance fall from the sky. It was a clear, sunny day. But the couple said it looked like large reddish-brown snowflakes were falling. After studying the fallen material, they thought it smelled and looked like meat. Several scientists who examined samples agreed that it was meat. One explanation for the meat shower is that it came from vultures flying overhead. Vultures sometimes vomit during flight, which may have caused pieces of meat to come raining down.

When the storage tank broke, the molasses swept forward in a giant wave. The wave reached 40 feet (12 m) high and surged through the streets at 35 miles per hour (56 kmh). The molasses covered everything in its path. It swept up people, horses, carts, houses, and even part of a train. It destroyed many businesses. Many people were injured by the debris the wave carried. Because the molasses was so thick, many people got stuck. Firefighters came to pull people out of the molasses.

The sticky flood killed 21 people and injured 150 more. The tank had burst because it was poorly constructed. The walls were too thin to hold the weight of the molasses. The tank had also not been tested for leaks. More than 100 people sued the company that owned the tank. They won their case and were awarded money for the damages they had suffered. This case changed construction standards, eventually making many structures across the country safer.

FURTHER EVIDENCE

Chapter Two discusses how food shapes historical events. What is the main point of this chapter? What key evidence supports this point? Go to the article below, which is about the importance of different cuisines. Find a quote from the website that supports the chapter's main point.

CUISINE

abdocorelibrary.com/weird-moments-history

CHAPTER THREE

WEIRD WARTIME MOMENTS

Wars are tragic events. They can cause huge losses of life. And they can destroy cities and even countries. In the midst of wartime violence, weird things have occurred.

During World War II (1939–1945), the United States was at war with Japan. US military leaders were looking for new strategies to help them win the war. One idea came from Pennsylvania dentist Lytle S. Adams. Adams thought about the thousands of bats he'd seen roosting in caves in

Lytle S. Adams saw a large swarm of bats fly out of a cave in search of food. It made him think about ways to use that behavior in war.

Franklin D. Roosevelt was president during the Great Depression (1929–1939) and World War II. He died in office shortly before the war's official end.

New Mexico. He wondered if the bats could be made into a new kind of weapon.

Adams wrote to President Franklin D. Roosevelt describing his plan. He proposed filling an empty bomb case with 1,000 bats. The bats would have explosive devices attached to their chests. Adams suggested that the case could be dropped by airplane over Japanese cities, where the bats would be released in a swarm. The bats would then roost in Japan's wooden buildings before exploding, causing widespread damage. Roosevelt decided to go forward with the idea.

A team began working on the bat bomb at an Army Air Corps base in New Mexico. The team captured thousands of bats and prepared a test. The bats were released from a plane, but the army had no control over where the bats went. The bats flew into buildings on the base. The devices exploded, and the buildings caught on fire. No people were injured, but the bat bomb was never used again.

THE ROSWELL INCIDENT

In the 1900s, people were so excited by the idea of alien life that reports of alien encounters made newspaper headlines. One of the most famous supposed alien encounters was the Roswell incident. In 1947, the US military released a secret spy balloon as part of a test. The balloon crashed near Roswell, New Mexico. Conflicting information about the origin of the balloon led some people to believe that it was an alien spacecraft. A local newspaper even printed an article describing the balloon as a flying saucer.

One rumor says Caligula, *center, giving cup to horse*, attempted to make his horse a consul, a high-ranking Roman position.

THE WAR ON THE SEA

Caligula was the Roman emperor between 37 and 41 CE. He is remembered as one of Rome's worst emperors. He was known for his cruel and erratic behaviors. He demanded to be worshipped as a god and executed many people. At age 29, he was assassinated by Rome's senators.

During his rule, Caligula declared war on an unusual enemy. One ancient biographer described Caligula leading his army to the shore of modern-day northern France. There, the emperor declared war on the sea and ordered his soldiers to attack the waves with their swords. He then ordered them to collect seashells, which he referred to as the spoils of war. Caligula declared victory over Neptune, the Roman god of the sea.

Some historians believe this event is evidence of Caligula being mentally unwell. Others say the attack was a show of authority over his army. No one knows Caligula's reasons for this so-called attack.

A WARTIME TRUCE

Wars involve battles and fighting but also a lot of waiting around. This was true during the American Civil War (1861–1865). In December 1862, the Union army and the Confederate army were encamped on either side of the Rappahannock River in Virginia. Soldiers from the opposing armies began to interact with each other. The Union army made toy boats filled with coffee and sent them across the river. The Confederate army sent back boats with tobacco and corn.

ANIMAL ANOMALIES

History mostly focuses on human events. But it can be hard to separate human history from the history of other animals. Humans domesticated animals for use as pets and livestock. Animal products such as meat, eggs, and milk have fed societies. Horses and oxen have served as pulling power and modes of transportation. But sometimes humans and animals have found themselves at odds with each other.

In the early 1930s, Australian farmers faced many challenges. The Australian government had

Veterinarian William Key trained a horse named Beautiful Jim Key. Jim could spell words, tell time, and do simple math.

Emus can sprint at speeds up to 30 miles per hour (50 kmh).

given land to veterans returning from World War I. But much of the land was located in a climate that made farming difficult. A severe drought in 1932 made matters even worse. Farmers struggled to produce crops. And they soon encountered yet another problem.

Emus are large flightless birds that live in Australia. They can grow up to 6 feet (1.8 m) tall and can weigh more than 100 pounds (45 kg). Emus often migrate in search of food in Australia's Outback. The Outback is the vast interior of Australia where very few people live. When the drought began, a flock of around 20,000 emus moved onto Australian farmland in search of food. They trampled and ate the wheat crops. The farmers installed barriers and used rifles to try to protect their fields. But the emus were quick and good at avoiding the farmers' shots.

THE EXPLODING WHALE

In 1970, a dead sperm whale washed up on the coast of Florence, Oregon. The whale was 45 feet (14 m) long and weighed 8 tons (7.3 metric tons). The rotting carcass was a health risk to the people living nearby. But they weren't sure how to get rid of it. Eventually, they decided to blow it up with dynamite. The explosion blew rotting whale chunks all over the beach and town. No one was harmed. People gathered the whale remains and buried them.

The farmers went to the Australian government for help. The government responded with its army. Soldiers used machine guns to fire at the emus. But the flocks would scatter in all directions, making them difficult targets. They were also good at hiding in the Outback's rough terrain. The government sent more troops and more guns. But the army had very limited success in the Emu War. It managed to kill only a few hundred of the 20,000 birds.

ANDREW JACKSON'S PARROT

Andrew Jackson was the seventh US president. He owned a beloved pet parrot named Poll. Jackson had given the parrot as a gift to his wife and continued to care for Poll after her death. Jackson passed away in 1845. The funeral was held at Jackson's home in Tennessee. One funeral attendee said that Poll was in attendance. But the bird had to be removed. The man wrote in a letter that the parrot caused a disruption by squawking and loudly swearing during the service.

NAPOLEON'S RABBIT ATTACK

Napoleon Bonaparte was a French general

The emperor of Russia in 1807 was Alexander I, whom Napoleon Bonaparte defeated in June of that year at the Battle of Friedland.

and emperor in the early 1800s. He was a brilliant military leader who won many battles. He expanded much of France's territory during the Napoleonic Wars (1801–1815). But there was one defeat he never saw coming. And it was not during battle.

In 1807, Bonaparte was celebrating a victory in battle against Russia. Part of the celebration was participating in a traditional rabbit hunt. Bonaparte's chief of staff arranged for a herd of rabbits to be

released from cages into a field. However, the rabbits did not run away when they were set free. Instead, they swarmed Bonaparte and his men. The domesticated rabbits were used to being fed by people. There were so many rabbits that Bonaparte and his men quickly became overwhelmed. The hunt was called off, and the field was left to the rabbits.

EXPLORE ONLINE

Chapter Four discusses humans' relationships with animals. The website below explores animal allies throughout history. As you know, every source is different. How is the information from the website different from the information in Chapter Four? What new information did you learn from the website?

ANIMAL HEROES

abdocorelibrary.com/weird-moments-history

Napoleon Bonaparte's many wartime victories have led him to be remembered as one of history's greatest military leaders.

CHAPTER FIVE

WILD WEATHER

People develop new technology to give them more control over their environment. For example, heating and cooling systems allow people to control the temperature of their homes and buildings. But weather is one thing that remains mostly out of human control. Some weird weather events in history have taken people by surprise.

In April 1815, a once-quiet volcano erupted with astounding force. The volcano was Mount Tambora in Indonesia. It was the largest volcano

Today, a lake occupies the crater left by Mount Tambora after its eruption. This lake sometimes dries up.

MOUNT TAMBORA'S ASH

This diagram shows approximately how much ash fell on the area surrounding Mount Tambora after the volcano erupted in 1815. What effects might the ash have had on people living on the nearby islands?

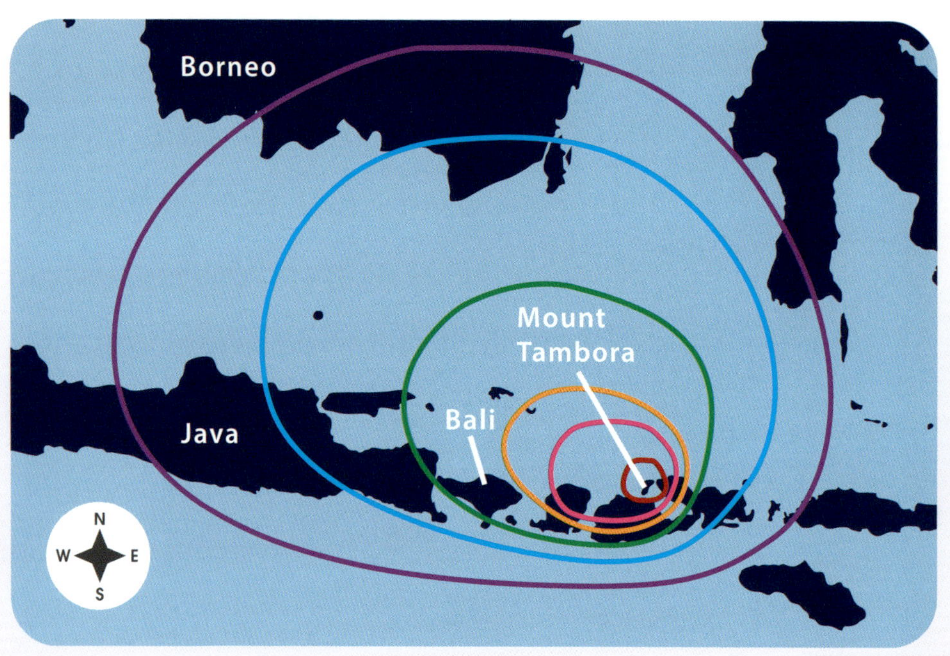

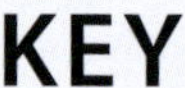

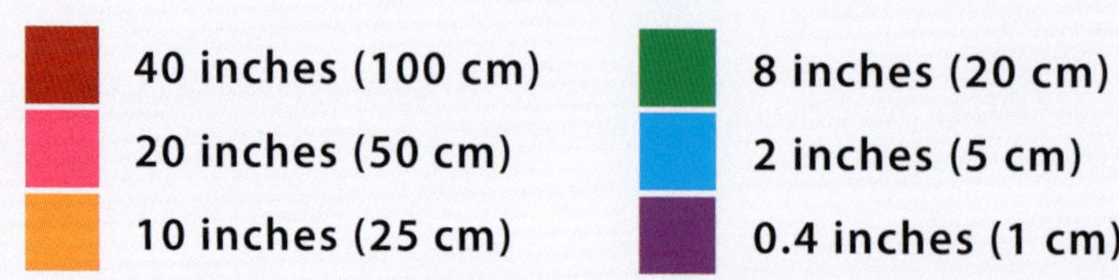

eruption in recorded history. Many people living near the volcano died. The violent eruption sent ash into the sky. Entire homes and towns were buried in ash. Several feet of ash coated the nearby oceans, and ships had to plow through it to pass.

The eruption released so much ash into the air that it temporarily blocked out the sun above the volcano. Over time, the ash spread throughout the atmosphere, affecting the entire planet. Global temperatures dropped. Parts of North America and Europe experienced snow and frost during the summer months.

WEATHER INSPIRATION

Gloomy weather during the year without a summer may have actually inspired classic works of art. In 1816, writers Mary Shelley, Lord Byron, and others were on vacation at Lake Geneva in Switzerland. Trapped indoors due to the weather, the writers competed to see who could write the best ghost story. Shelley wrote her famous novel *Frankenstein* during the competition. The novel features dark and stormy weather much like what Shelley lived through that summer.

The year 1816 became known as "the year without a summer."

The colder temperatures had destructive effects on food production. Many crops died, and food became much scarcer in some parts of the world. This caused the price of food to rise, leading to disorder and civil unrest. Soon the temporary effects of the volcano began to ease. Particles of ash in the atmosphere slowly fell back to Earth.

A CITY UNDERWATER

The greatest flood of the 1900s happened in 1910 in Paris, France. After an extremely rainy summer and autumn, water levels rose higher than they ever had. The flood lasted for two months, and most of the Paris streets were underwater. Thousands of people evacuated the city, and five people died. Engineers built wooden walkways above the water so that people could get around. Others used boats to row through the city's streets.

A RECORD TEMPERATURE SWING

Montana is known for its cold temperatures. The lowest temperature recorded

Warm winds that blow down the eastern side of the Rocky Mountains are called chinook winds.

in Montana was −70 degrees Fahrenheit (−57°C). But in 1972, a different kind of record was set. On the morning of January 14, a man named Jim Wood noted the temperature outside his home in Loma, Montana. It was −54 degrees Fahrenheit (−48°C).

That night, southwest winds blew into Loma. The winds reached speeds of 30 to 40 miles per hour (50–65 kmh). The winds warmed as they blew down the Rocky Mountains, causing a rapid rise in temperature. The next morning, on January 15, Wood checked the temperature again. This time, it was 49 degrees Fahrenheit (9°C). This meant that in a period of 24 hours, the temperature had changed by 103 degrees Fahrenheit (58°C). This set a world record for the biggest temperature swing in recorded history.

History is the story of humanity's past. But that story is more than what is found in books, movies, and television shows. Moments in history may be mysterious or hard to explain. And some are so weird that they continue to surprise historians today.

STRAIGHT TO THE
SOURCE

Sir Thomas Stamford Raffles was a British colonial official on the island of Java. He was only about 800 miles (1,290 km) away from Mount Tambora when it erupted. He described the event in a letter:

> *On the evening of the 10th the explosions became very loud; one in particular shook the town, and they were excessively quick, resembling [heavy cannon fire]. Towards evening, next day, the atmosphere thickened so much, that by four o'clock it was necessary to light candles. . . . The uncommon darkness of this night did not break till ten and eleven, A.M. of the 12th, and it could hardly be called day-light all day. Volcanic ashes fell in abundance, and covered the earth about two inches thick, the trees also were loaded with them.*

Source: Sophia Hull. *Memoir of the Life and Public Services of Sir Thomas Stamford Raffles*. London: John Murray, 1830, p. 243.

WHAT'S THE BIG IDEA?

Take a close look at this passage. How does Raffles describe the eruption of Mount Tambora? Do the details help you imagine what it might have been like to experience?

FAST FACTS

- Historical coincidences intrigue historians. One historical coincidence is that John Adams and Thomas Jefferson both died on July 4, 1826.
- French people were hesitant to try potatoes after the vegetables had been introduced to Europe. Antoine-Augustin Parmentier pretended that potatoes were highly valuable to change people's minds.
- Food can shape history in unexpected ways. A molasses flood in Boston led to an improvement in construction standards across the United States.
- The US military explored using bats to fly bombs into enemy cities during World War II.
- Roman emperor Caligula once ordered his army to attack the sea.
- In 1932, Australian emus were feeding on farmers' limited crops. The Australian military attempted to kill the emus in what became known as the Emu War.

- Renowned military leader Napoleon Bonaparte was once swarmed by a group of rabbits while trying to hunt.
- A volcano eruption in Indonesia temporarily lowered global temperatures, causing "the year without a summer" in 1816.
- The world record for the largest one-day temperature swing occurred in Loma, Montana. The temperature changed by 103 degrees Fahrenheit (58°C) in one day.

STOP AND THINK

Tell the Tale

Chapter Two of this book discusses the Great Molasses Flood in Boston. Imagine you are in Boston at the time. Write 200 words about what you see.

Say What?

Studying history can mean learning a lot of new vocabulary. Find five words in this book you've never heard before. Use a dictionary to find out what they mean. Then write the meanings in your own words and use each word in a new sentence.

Surprise Me

Chapter Three discusses weird moments in the history of war. After reading this book, what two or three facts about weird war history did you find most surprising? Write a few sentences about each fact. Why did you find each fact surprising?

Another View

This book talks about the eruption of Mount Tambora in April 1815. As you know, every source is different. Ask a librarian or another adult to help you find another source about this event. Write a short essay comparing and contrasting the new source's point of view with that of this book's author. What is the point of view of each author? How are they similar and why? How are they different and why?

GLOSSARY

assassinate
to kill someone for political or religious reasons

atmosphere
the gases that surround Earth

bribe
a gift of money given to influence a person in power

coincidence
events that happen at the same time that seem to be connected

cultivate
to care for growing plants to use as food

debris
scattered waste or material

diplomat
a person who represents a country outside the country

domesticate
to tame a living thing for human use

economics
the study of the production of goods and services

erratic
irregular and unpredictable

stewardess
a woman who takes care of passengers' needs, such as serving food

sue
to seek legal action against a person or company after being wronged

veteran
a person who has served in the military

ONLINE RESOURCES

To learn more about weird moments in history, visit our free resource websites below.

Visit **abdocorelibrary.com** or scan this QR code for free Common Core resources for teachers and students, including vetted activities, multimedia, and booklinks, for deeper subject comprehension.

Visit **abdobooklinks.com** or scan this QR code for free additional online weblinks for further learning. These links are routinely monitored and updated to provide the most current information available.

LEARN MORE

Buckey, A. W. *Weird Experiments*. Abdo, 2026.

Mihaly, Christy. *The Haunted History of Washington, DC*. Abdo, 2024.

The World War II Book. DK, 2022.

INDEX

About the Author

Emma Kaiser is a writer and educator based in western Minnesota. She has a master of fine arts in creative writing from the University of Minnesota, and her writing has appeared in a number of magazines and publications. She is the author of many nonfiction books for students and loves watching historical documentaries.